ACTIVITIES FOR

FAST FINISHERS

Vocabulary

by Marc Tyler Nobleman

SCHOLASTIC
PROFESSIONAL BOOKS

New York • Toronto • London • Auckland • Sydney
Mexico City • New Delhi • Hong Kong • Buenos Aires

Edited by Denise Willi
Cover design by Maria Lilja
Cover illustration by Jeff Shelly
Interior illustrations by Steve Cox, Anne Kennedy, Mike Moran, and Jared Lee
Interior design by Melinda Belter

ISBN: 0-439-41122-X
Copyright © 2002 by Marc Tyler Nobleman
All rights reserved.
Printed in the U.S.A.

3 4 5 6 7 8 9 10   40   09 08 07 06 05 04 03

FAST FINISHERS

Vocabulary

Contents

Teacher Letter

About This Book

It happens to teachers all the time. A class is taking a test or working on a project and a few students finish sooner than the rest. They're sitting around, looking bored. What can you give them so they'll use what's left of the period in a valuable and enriching way?

That's where this book can be of help. It's full of high-interest activities that your students are sure to love. Does your class like crossword puzzles? What about word finds? Jumbles?

If so, they'll love the activities in this book, though none is a conventional crossword puzzle, word find, or jumble. In many instances, these exercises take those activities and add a twist—or just stand them on their head.

Meanwhile, *you'll* like the activities in this book because they reinforce your curriculum by focusing on vocabulary, word study skills, dictionary skills, and more, in fun new ways. There are even activities that sneak in a little science, social studies, and math. There are 55 one-page activities in all, designed to be worked on independently for an average of ten to fifteen minutes each. We've provided a checklist on the next page so you, and your students, can track which activities they've completed.

This book doesn't back down from challenging kids. It doesn't always go with the familiar word. It doesn't lose its effect if it makes a student want to look up a word in a reference source—in fact, all the better. It prefers not to repeat approaches, but if it does, then it must be for good reason! I hope you and your students enjoy this book.

— *Marc Tyler Nobleman*

Name _____

Student Checklist

Vocabulary

Track Your Progress!

Put a ✓ in the box for each activity you complete.

Date _____

Name _____

FAST
FINISHERS

Vocabulary

Not Your Usual Crossword

Unlike most crossword puzzles, the crossword below already has the words filled in. Your job is to find the clue that belongs to each word and write it in the appropriate blank below. Beware! There are more clues than words in the puzzle. We've done the first one for you.

CLUES

- mythical creature
- not a vowel
- table
- dish for cereal
- VCR
- sphere
- country
- a group of three
- dinner
- transmit document by phone line
- regular
- to prevent something
- circle
- hot breakfast
- a secret plan
- large land mass
- strange
- not take part in

¹C	²O	N	³T	I	N	E	⁴N	T
	A		R				O	
	T		I		⁵O	R	B	
	M		O	⁶P		M		
	E			L		A		
	A		⁷F	O	I	L		
⁸E	L	⁹F		T				
		A						
	¹⁰E	X	E	M	P	T		

ACROSS	DOWN
1. *large land mass*	2. _____
5. _____	3. _____
7. _____	4. _____
8. _____	6. _____
10. _____	9. _____

FAST FINISHERS

Vocabulary

Can You Smell a Rat?

Is *rodotephobia* (fear of rodents) a real word, or not? Believe it or not, every word in each group of words below is in the dictionary—except for one. Choose the fake word and write it in the blank. Guess if you don't know, then check the dictionary—if it's not there, you were correct!

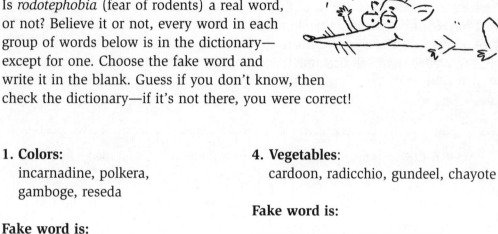

1. Colors:
incarnadine, polkera, gamboge, reseda

Fake word is:

_____

2. Animals:
potto, jerboa, onager, kloogus

Fake word is:

_____

3. Countries:
Bhutan, Scotzygan, Djibouti, Qatar

Fake word is:

_____

4. Vegetables:
cardoon, radicchio, gundeel, chayote

Fake word is:

_____

5. Punctuation marks:
siltic, macron, dieresis, breve

Fake word is:

_____

6. Phobias:
rodotephobia (fear of rodents), catoptrophobia (fear of mirrors), pteronophobia (fear of being tickled by feathers), agrizoophobia (fear of wild animals)

Fake word is:

_____

YOUR TURN

Use two of the challenging words above in a sentence and demonstrate your language power!

_____

_____

_____

FAST FINISHERS

Vocabulary

Date _____

Name _____

The One Word

There's a 12-letter mystery word hiding in the center of this puzzle that describes a type of person. To figure it out, look at the list of 12-letter words in the box below. Only one will fill each letter box in the column *and* complete the words in all the rows. Which word is it? The words in the puzzle will also give you clues about this type of person.

WORD LIST:	psychologist	cartographer	statistician
	speleologist	salutatorian	somnambulist
	caricaturist	philanthropist	seismologist

1.				h	e	e	t s
2.	s	n	o	z	e		
3.	d	r	e	a			
4.			s	o	r	e	
5.			n	p			
6.	p	a j	a	a	s		
7.				l	a	n k e t	
8.		s	h	t	e	y e	
9.		p	i	l	o	w	
10.			m	d	n	i g	h t
11.				l	e	e p y	
12.	b	e	d	i	m	e	

The mystery word describes a type of person. Do you know what this person does? Write your best guess then check it in a dictionary.

_____

_____

_____

FAST FINISHERS

Date _____

Name _____

Vocabulary

You're Breaking Up

If you break up the word *snapshot* and rearrange some letters, you can make two new words: *hops* and *ants*. All the words below can be broken into two smaller words. Use the clues to help you figure out which words and write them in the chart. Every letter in the bigger word is used only once to make the two smaller words.

BIGGER WORD	CLUE 1	SMALLER WORD 1	CLUE 2	SMALLER WORD 2
1. doorbell	you wear it in the morning to keep warm		child's toy that often can be dressed up	
2. airplane	bucket		not far	
3. something	phantom		not yours	
4. password	stinging insect		thin metal bars	
5. roommate	not less		water surrounding a castle	
6. sweetheart	to use thread to make clothing		where you see a film or a play	
7. outburst	to travel in a foreign country		to bang your toe	
8. snowflake	slithering animal		to move like water	

YOUR TURN

Find a word of seven letters or more that you can break into two smaller words.

_____   _____   _____

FAST FINISHERS

Vocabulary

Date _____

Name _____

The Name Game

Each of these people, animals, places, or things needs a name. Based on the item's description, circle which name would be the best fit and give your reason. You may consult a dictionary for help. We've done the first one for you.

Item 1: A rock band that wears only green clothes and dyes their hair green

Best Name: Ruby or (Emerald?)

Emerald is the better name because it is a shade of green. Ruby is a shade of red.

Item 2: A computer model that promises greater speed

Best Name: Inertia 3000 or Velocity 3000?

_____

_____

Item 3: A travel agency that specializes in trips to the country

Best Name: Cosmopolitan Travel or Provincial Travel?

_____

_____

Item 4: A book about comedy

Best Name: *Monarch's Handbook* or *Jester's Handbook*?

_____

_____

Item 5: A hotel that promises a peaceful and quiet stay

Best Name: Turbulence Inn or Tranquility Inn?

_____

_____

Item 6: A dog who is very well behaved

Best Name: Chaos or Etiquette?

_____

_____

Item 7: A town with strong cultural diversity

Best Name: Mosaic or Uniform?

_____

_____

Item 8: A concert hall with great acoustics

Best Name: Muffle Hall or Resonate Hall?

_____

_____

Item 9: Toothpaste that glows in the dark

Best Name: Opaque Gel or Luminous Gel?

_____

_____

Item 10: A recently discovered type of dinosaur that was very small

Best Name: Microscoposaurus or Colossasaurus?

_____

_____

FAST FINISHERS

Vocabulary

Date _____

Name _____

Jumbled and Incomplete

Each group contains three jumbled words, but each jumbled word is missing one letter. In fact, all the words in a group are missing the *same* letter. Use the clues to figure out that missing letter, add it to each jumble, and unscramble the words. The first one is done for you.

JUMBLED WORDS	CLUES	LETTER TO ADD TO EACH WORD	UNSCRAMBLED WORDS
1. dana, ciner, zerelt	type of bear, royal son, knotted bread snack	*P*	*panda, prince, pretzel*
2. mare, zilzer, staint	story while sleeping, light rain, far away		
3. bleg, brawin, nerujy	miniature model of the Earth, multi-colored arc of light, trip		
4. chea, vear, noirg	sandy land near sea, courageous, dull		
5. lkm, trenw, leccyb	white drink, cold season, two-wheeled vehicle		
6. tome, roart, raterue	a bright heavenly body with a long tail of light, orange vegetable, animal		
7. koe, gleun, gelgu	short funny story or prank, hot climate with lots of plants and animals, toss and keep several objects in the air at once		
8. orc, seran, psierh	black bird, respond to question, talk softly		

YOUR TURN

Create a word jumble of your own, with clues, like the ones above. Test it on your classmates to see if they can figure it out.

FAST FINISHERS

Vocabulary

Date _____

Name _____

Rhyme With Reason

Each word below is missing some consonants. Use the clues to figure out which ones, and write them in the blanks. All the missing consonants throughout the entire activity rhyme. Each consonant can be used more than once. We've done the first one for you.

WORD THAT NEEDS RHYMING CONSONANTS	CLUE
1. _d_ o _z_ e	sleep
2. ___ra___e	red or green fruit
3. ___o___y___uar___	someone who protects someone else
4. ___la___e	fire
5. ___e___e___a___le	type of healthy food
6. in___a___e	enter another country to attack
7. ___ar___e___	something you aim for
8. a___ ___i___e	good suggestion
9. ___au___e	used in a bandage
10. ___e___ar___	leave

ANSWERS:

1. _d, z – doze_

2. _____

3. _____

4. _____

5. _____

6. _____

7. _____

8. _____

9. _____

10. _____

FAST FINISHERS

Vocabulary

Date _____

Name _____

Fall Back or Spring Ahead?

Below is a series of questions. The answers are also here, but they're in code! To break the code, change each letter in the answer to either the letter that comes before it in the alphabet or after it. Keep changing letters until you get the right word. We've done the first one for you.

HINT Each letter may have a different code in different words or even within the same word. For example, *g* may be coded as *f* in one instance and *h* in another—even in the same word.

1. What did Jack of fairy tale fame climb?
afbotsbkl = ___*beanstalk*___

2. What is a mineral deposit that hangs from a cave ceiling called?

rsbmbbujsf = _____

3. What is a synonym for weak?

gddamd = _____

4. What is half the earth called?

ifnjtogdsf = _____

5. What word describes an object that is so clear that light passes through it?
usborqbqfou = _____

6. Someone who helps a criminal is called what?
bbbpnokjdd = _____

7. What is another word for seawater?

csjof = _____

8. A song performed by voice only (without any instruments) is performed how?
bdboqdmmb = _____

9. Something that is small can be described as what?
ehnhmvsjwf = _____

10. A platypus can also be called what other name?

evblajkm = _____

YOUR TURN

Write a question with the answer encoded like the examples above. See if your classmates can figure out the answer.

FAST FINISHERS

VOCABULARY

Date _____

Name _____

Letters on the Run

Be a letter wrangler! Round up the escaping consonants from the "runaway letters" column, then reunite them with their vowels in the "words missing consonants" column.

Here's how to do it. The vowels in the first column are in the correct order that they appear in the word. Look at the clues (including the total number of letters in the complete word), then take a guess at the word. Plug in the consonants (each one belongs to a word, but they're not in any order in the column) to confirm your guess, and cross each one out as you use it. (Use a pencil so you can erase in case you need to try a different consonant.) Write your completed words in the blanks below.

WORDS MISSING CONSONANTS	CLUE	TOTAL NUMBER OF LETTERS IN COMPLETE WORD	RUNAWAY LETTERS
1. oai	green spot with water in the desert	5	v r n t c
2. eeie	spooky	5	c p w
3. iie	spear of frozen water that hangs from roofs	6	s c n m
4. ei	to scroll back a cassette videotape	6	d c p l d
5. oa	area where apples grow	7	r r r
6. oe	to guard	7	r l c h
7. ao	big net swing hung in back yard to relax in	7	t k s
8. eeoe	paper enclosure in which you put a letter	8	m h

1. _____   5. _____

2. _____   6. _____

3. _____   7. _____

4. _____   8. _____

FAST FINISHERS

Vocabulary

Date _____

Name _____

EE-ther OAr

The letters on the list of consonant combinations below are waiting to become words. All you need to do is insert the vowel combination "ee" and "oa" somewhere in the middle, without changing the order of the consonants. But watch out! Not all of the words that you will create are real. Circle only the consonant combinations that form words with both vowel combinations. Write *yes* only if both words are real; otherwise write *no*. Explain your choice in the blanks below. We've done the first two for you.

1. (td)   *yes (teed, toad)*
2. ct   *no (ceet, coat)*
3. ft _____
4. mn _____
5. sr _____
6. flt _____
7. mt _____
8. sd _____
9. slt _____
10. bt _____
11. rr _____
12. tr _____
13. sk _____
14. pk _____
15. crk _____

YOUR TURN

Think of five more consonant combinations like the ones above. Then test them by inserting "ee" or "oa" and tell whether they are real words.

___   _____
___   _____
___   _____
___   _____
___   _____

15

FAST FINISHERS

Vocabulary

Date _____

Name _____

Four Squares

There are several hidden words in each grid, but only
four are based on each grid's clue. Circle those four. Words
are across or down, not diagonal or backward. Good luck!

```
l  o  b  s  t  e  r  u
o  y  i  w  a  v  k  e
s  l  t  w  l  o  o  e
t  l  j  a  c  k  a  l
r  a  b  a  r  p  l  p
i  m  u  s  k  r  a  t
c  a  h  s  n  a  k  e
h  z  e  o  w  a  s  p
```

Grid 1 Clue: mammals

```
b  g  s  h  e  l  f  l
o  o  l  s  d  a  s  i
o  m  o  v  i  e  p  b
k  b  m  a  s  j  i  r
m  n  y  p  l  e  n  a
a  c  h  a  p  t  e  r
r  a  q  g  u  c  v  y
k  p  r  e  f  a  c  e
```

Grid 2 Clue: parts of a book

```
q  e  c  u  a  d  o  r
f  y  p  r  w  e  x  c
r  t  c  u  b  a  i  h
a  o  i  g  h  u  n  i
n  l  y  u  g  o  d  l
c  i  z  a  i  r  i  e
e  o  u  y  f  a  a  y
b  o  l  i  v  i  a  i
```

Grid 3 Clue: South American countries

```
c  y  j  k  e  i  b  o
r  e  m  e  r  a  l  d
i  z  c  l  f  l  n  t
m  a  z  l  u  b  e  h
s  v  h  y  j  l  b  e
o  h  o  r  a  g  o  x
n  e  a  w  d  s  n  i
o  l  i  v  e  a  y  p
```

Grid 4 Clue: shades of green

FAST FINISHERS

Vocabulary

Date _____

Name _____

Out of Here!

One item on each list below actually belongs in
another list. To get the item "out of here," circle it.
Then write the number of the list where it really belongs.
When you're done, write what each list is about. The first
one is done for you.

LIST	CIRCLED WORD BELONGS ON LIST #?	WHAT IS THIS LIST ABOUT?
1. thigh, (cylinder,) calf	6	*parts of a leg*
2. slingshot, pavement, tomahawk		
3. pond, palette, lagoon		
4. bog, town, village		
5. jaguar, panther, creek		
6. cube, sphere, triathlon		
7. swamp, marsh, puma		
8. easel, canvas, catapult		
9. blacktop, hamlet, asphalt		
10. decathlon, marathon, shin		

YOUR TURN

Create a chart of your own like the one above but using only four lists.
See whether a classmate can figure out which item doesn't belong, where
it should go, and what each list is all about.

Date _____

Name _____

FAST FINISHERS

Vocabulary

Say What?

The answer to each question is hidden in the word find below. Circle only words that are answers, although other dummy answers are hidden to throw you off! Words are across or down, forward or backward, but not diagonal. Write the correct and dummy answers in the chart.

QUESTION	ANSWER	DUMMY ANSWERS (DON'T CIRCLE)
1. How many days are in a fortnight?		
2. Your collarbone is also called what?		
3. What are the "[ ]" punctuation marks called?		
4. Feline is to cat as what is to cow?		
5. What was a Russian ruler formerly called?		
6. What is a tropical cyclone otherwise known as?		
7. "Arachnophobia" is fear of what?		
8. What is a one-word way to say "three times"?		

HINT Not all questions have dummy answers.

WORD FIND

```
R O W H I R L P O O L D T X
A P S T E R N U M S U A Y O
Z L T O M A B T I A V R P E
C P E R U B E H J N F K H L
T H K N F O U R T E E N O C
W A C A T V R I L F M P O I
E R A D R I S C D U U A N V
L A R O W N T E E R R I T A
V O B S R E D I P S O S H L
E H E F O R T Y K I N G A C
H E I G H T S C A N I N E U
A I P A R E N T H E S E S I
```

Date _____

Name _____

Change Is in the Air

Each sentence below contains a boldface word and a missing word. To figure out the missing word, you'll need to look at the context of the words around it and change some letters in the boldface word. The numbers in parentheses indicate how many letters must change to get the correct answer. The tips will help you out, too. We've done the first one for you.

HELPFUL TIPS:
* Each new word has the same number of letters as the original word.
* Letters are not rearranged but rather replaced with other letters.
* The words don't have to rhyme, but they might.

1. I lost my bike **lock** because I always have bad ___luck___. (1)

2. My **horse** is very well behaved, but my parents still won't let me bring him in the _____. (1)

3. It's easy to see the **moon** at midnight, but not so easy at _____. (1)

4. Whoever is not the **winner** has to cook _____ for the rest of us. (1)

5. People might stare if you walk down the **sidewalk** _____ instead of facing forward. (2)

6. The waves **crashed** onto the deck of the sloop with such force they _____ out some of the boat's windows. (2)

7. Can you see a **shadow** reflected in a _____? (3)

8. The crook snuck into the library and **took** the rare and valuable _____. (1)

9. That **puzzle** is so hard that it took six _____ working together to finish it. (3)

10. Coming to school with **stripes** painted on your face is indeed a bit _____. (4)

11. When the **hen** saw the fox in the distance she got so scared she ran straight into the wire mesh _____ for safety. (1)

12. When the neighbor came to **return** our lost cat, my mother fetched the _____ money from her dresser. (4)

YOUR TURN

Write a sentence with a missing word and a boldface word like the ones above. See if your classmates can figure it out by changing the number of letters you've indicated inside the parentheses.

19

Date _____

Name _____

Definition Plugs

Each boldface word is defined, but a word from its definition is missing.
To find the missing word, look at the other boldface words on the list.
Pick the correct one based on clues about the missing word in the sentence.
Each boldface word will plug into only one definition. We've done one for you.

1. **farm** —a piece of _____*land*_____ used to grow crops

2. **grammar** —the rules of speaking or writing a _____

3. **orchestra** —a large group of musicians who play their instruments
   together (often in a _____ orchestra, which usually plays
   classical music)

4. **land** —solid _____

5. **music** —the art of arranging sounds to _____ a melody,
   harmony, or rhythm

6. **pencil** —a narrow _____ used for writing or drawing made of
   a thin rod of graphite covered in wood

7. **period** —a punctuation mark that is used to end a sentence, consisting
   of a single dot (easily made from the tip of a _____ !)

8. **grasp** —to _____ something and hold it tightly

9. **young** —being at an early _____ in life

10. **language** —the words and _____ that people use to talk and
    write to each other

11. **ground** —to punish someone, especially a _____ person,
    by making him or her stay at home

12. **seize** —to _____ or take hold of something suddenly

13. **produce** —fresh fruits and vegetables from a _____

14. **symphony** —a large _____ that usually plays classical music

15. **instrument** —a device used to play _____

Date _____

Name _____

Vocabulary

E-ttachments

Read the e-mail from Tim to his friend Jan. Circle any words that can form new words when an "e" is added to the end—or beginning. If an applicable word appears more than once, you only have to circle it the first time. Proper names count!

Hi Jan,

Sorry it took me so long to write back. My family just got back from a trip to Lake Erie. We rode through New York, Pennsylvania, and Ohio and ended up in the great state of Michigan. My parents have been there in the past but my sister and I never have. One of the most spectacular things we saw was a huge migration of birds over the water. We stayed up late the whole week. The sky was so clear you could see a star in any direction. It could get very cold, worse than sitting next to an air conditioner vent. Sometimes we would sit on a bench at the shore and hug each other to stay warm! Once we saw some motion in the water and thought we saw the fin of some large animal, but it was just a breeze blowing over the surface. It was dusk and the daylight was so dim that you couldn't blame us for it! It was nice to be someplace where you can hear gentle waves lapping all night. There were a ton of people on vacation there, though the crowd included a whole unit of police officers. They were having some kind of conference. I stood next to one of them in line at the buffet and she asked if I was having a good time. Of course, I said yes. She looked at my plate of food and quipped, "I knew you'd say that—I've never seen so much food on such a small plate. Where does a small, bony person like you fit all of that food?" I laughed so much that I dropped my fork, and it rang when it hit the floor. I must have looked so clumsy to her.

You should definitely go sometime!

Your friend,
Tim

YOUR TURN

Go back to the last e-mail or letter you wrote or received. Try to find words that could either begin or end with an added "e."

FAST finishers

Date _____

Name _____

Vocabulary

One Word, Two Words

Each compound word below is followed by a list
of four more words. Each of those four words is
associated with either the first or the second word
in the compound word. They can be a type of one
of the words, a part of one of them, or a synonym for one of them.
Write which each is in the chart below. We've done the first one for you.

	break	fast
1. breakfast: breakneck, rift, rupture, rash	*rift, rupture*	*breakneck, rash*
	light	**house**
2. lighthouse: abode, luminous, spectrum, domicile		
	gold	**fish**
3. goldfish: bullion, karat, cod, grouper		
	flower	**pot**
4. flowerpot: orchid, cauldron, kettle, geranium		
	bed	**rock**
5. bedrock: slate, obsidian, trundle, futon		
	red	**head**
6. redhead: cranium, crimson, noggin, rouge		
	play	**mate**
7. playmate: frolic, partner, romp, associate		
	under	**take**
8. undertake: get, beneath, subterranean, secure		

22

FAST FINISHERS

Vocabulary

Date _____

Name _____

Inside Information

Look at the items in column A of the chart below. Every one of them is commonly found *inside* one item in column B. Match the appropriate pairs and write your answers on the blanks below. There is only one correct letter match for each numbered item. We've done the first one for you.

COLUMN A	COLUMN B	CORRECT MATCH
1. butter	**a.** balloon	*1. e*
2. coin	**b.** pantry	_____
3. pupil	**c.** vault	_____
4. pig	**d.** shed	_____
5. helium	**e.** refrigerator	_____
6. cereal	**f.** sty	_____
7. assets	**g.** fountain	_____
8. rake	**h.** eye	_____
9. license	**i.** bottle	_____
10. arrow	**j.** mirror	_____
11. battery	**k.** flashlight	_____
12. mercury	**l.** quiver	_____
13. reflection	**m.** thermometer	_____
14. lint	**n.** wallet	_____
15. message	**o.** dryer	_____

YOUR TURN

Think of five more items commonly found inside another item like in the chart above. Mix them up and see if your classmates can pair them together correctly.

FAST FINISHERS

Date _____

Name _____

Vocabulary

Double the Fun

This year Woodland Elementary School didn't have time to conduct both the annual spelling bee and the geography bee as they usually do, so they combined them. Read each student's answers in the chart below. Check "yes" if the answer is totally correct. If not, check "no" and explain what's wrong. Then, write the correct answer. If you're not sure of a fact, make your best guess then check it in a reference book. Be careful! Sometimes both the spelling *and* geography might be wrong. The first one is done for you.

QUESTION	STUDENT'S ANSWER	YES	NO	YOUR ANSWER
1. What is the name of the world's largest island?	Cuba		✓	*geography is wrong; should be Greenland*
2. What is the highest mountain in Africa?	Kilimanjaro			
3. Cairo is the capital of what country?	Ejypt			
4. Which is the smallest of North America's Great Lakes?	Ontario			
5. What is America's longest river?	Misisipi			
6. What is the highest mountain the world?	Kiliminjaro			
7. Three U.S. state capitals begin with the letter "J." They are Jackson, Jefferson City, and what?	Junaeu			
8. What is China's capital, Peking, more commonly called?	Shanghai			
9. The southernmost city in the world is Ushuaia, in what country?	Argentina			
10. Great Britain comprises England, Scotland, Wales, and what fourth country?	Finland			

It All Adds Up

Answer the puzzle questions below and then shade each answer's letters in the grid. Make sure you spell out all numbers. When you're finished, the unshaded boxes can be rearranged to answer the mystery question.

PUZZLE QUESTIONS

1. What unit of measure is abbreviated as *m*? _____

2. What is the name of the period used in a number to show that all the numbers to its right are less than 1? _____

3. What is the other common temperature measuring system besides Fahrenheit? _____

4. How many years are there in three-quarters of a century? _____

5. What is a shape with eight sides called? _____

6. What is the first written number in the English language to contain the letter "a"? _____

MYSTERY QUESTION

What is a number that is subtracted from another number called?

Answer _____

PUZZLE GRID

I	C	T	D	M	O	E	I	I	T
P	V	U	E	E	S	F	M	L	C
C	T	N	N	T	N	T	D	E	O
E	G	V	N	O	E	E	R	A	T
E	A	H	S	A	A	S	B	R	H
L	Y	U	I	S	D	N	U	O	S

FAST FINISHERS

Vocabulary

Date _____

Name _____

Blue Moon

How many words are there to describe a shade of blue? What are the names of some of the moons in our solar system? The list of names below will test how much you know. Next to each one, write "blue" or "moon" and the name of the planet it belongs to (if you know). If you're stumped, make your best guess. Then check your answers in a reference book.

NAME	BLUE OR MOON?	PLANET?
1. indigo		
2. callisto		
3. deimos		
4. cobalt		
5. cerulean		
6. charon		
7. cyan		
8. azure		
9. oberon		
10. titan		

YOUR TURN

Pick a shade of blue or a moon from the list above and write a sentence using that word. Or, if you dare, try to use both a shade of blue and a moon in a zany sentence or paragraph.

_____

_____

_____

_____

Date _____

Name _____

The Class Is All Ears

To learn about the human body, every student
in science class was assigned to learn about one
particular organ or body part and share what he or
she learned in an oral report. Based on the clues, what was
each student assigned?

STUDENT	CLUES	ORGAN OR BODY PART
1. Andrew	• we have two • on the outside • they have "soles"	
2. Maxine	• we have one • on the inside • it has "buds"	
3. Paul	• we have one • on the inside • it has "lobes"	
4. Bethany	• we have two • on the outside • they have "lobes"	
5. Yael	• we have two • on the outside • they have "cones"	
6. Jason	• we have one • on the inside • it has "valves"	
7. Dan	• we have two • on the inside • they have "sacs"	
8. Leslie	• we have many more than two • on the inside • they have "roots"	

YOUR TURN

Choose a body part that is not used above and create a list of clues for it.
See if a classmate can use your clues to guess the correct part.

27

FAST FINISHERS

Vocabulary

State of the Art

A new exhibit by the mysterious "Alphabet Painter" is touring the country's art museums this year. The painter has written clues to indicate which states he wants his paintings to visit each month. To figure out which states, look at the set of clues for each month below. Write your best guess in the blank. Then use an atlas or other reference materials to see whether you were correct.

HINT: Not every state will receive a visit

MONTH	ALPHABET PAINTER'S CLUES	STATES
1. January	all states ending in "y"	
2. February	all states whose names begin with a letter that no other state name begins with	
3. March	all states whose names have only one consonant or one syllable	
4. April	all states that begin and end with "A"	
5. May	all states that contain another state name within it, in order	
6. June	all states that begin and end with two different vowels	
7. July	all states whose names have only two consonants	
8. August	all states whose names have only two syllables	
9. September	states with consecutive double consonants	
10. October	states whose first two letters are consonants	
11. November	all states beginning with "N" except those whose first word is "New"	
12. December	states with consecutive double vowels	

Date _____

Name _____

Vocabulary

All Mixed Up

The items in each chart below are all mixed up. They belong in either one of two categories. Figure out what the categories are, then place a check in the appropriate column. We've started the first one for you.

CHART 1

WORDS	CATEGORY 1: *outside of the body*	CATEGORY 2:
thumbnail	*thumbnail*	
capillary		
eyelash	*eyelash*	
scalp		
esophagus		
temple		

CHART 2

WORDS	CATEGORY 1:	CATEGORY 2:
Jefferson		
Edison		
Reagan		
Wilson		
Carver		
Wright		

CHART 3

WORDS	CATEGORY 1:	CATEGORY 2:
canyon		
mountain		
gorge		
hilltop		
ravine		
crest		

Date _____

Name _____

Vocabulary

Earth, Wind, and Fire

Each word below is associated with one of the four elements: air, earth, fire, or water. The elements are represented by four icons below. Draw a line from the word to its most appropriate icon.

WORDS

1. topsoil
2. inferno
3. tide
4. cultivate
5. cloud
6. combustible
7. dew
8. oxygen
9. atmosphere
10. ember
11. condensation
12. arid
13. altitude
14. molten
15. crust

ELEMENTS

Air

Earth

Fire

Water

YOUR TURN

Think of three more words associated with air, earth, fire, or water.
Ask your classmates to think of the meaning of each word and name its most appropriate element.

Date _____

Name _____

Vocabulary

From This to That

Below are three lists of words that have to do with geography, history, and math. You'll need to know the meaning of the words in order to rank them as indicated. If you need help, use a dictionary or other reference source.

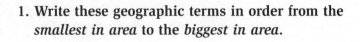

1. **Write these geographic terms in order from the** *smallest in area* **to the** *biggest in area.*

   city   _____

   county   _____

   continent   _____

   town   _____

   hemisphere   _____

2. **Write these historical figures in order from** *earliest time period* **to** *most recent time period.*

   medieval knight   _____

   Pilgrim   _____

   Neanderthal   _____

   Roman gladiator   _____

   Viking   _____

3. **Write these number words from** *least in amount* **to** *greatest in amount.*

   gross   _____

   dozen   _____

   million   _____

   billion   _____

   score   _____

FAST FINISHERS

Vocabulary

Date _____

Name _____

Amazing Science

In the box below is a list of scientific terms. Each word falls under one category in the chart. Write the word in the appropriate column.

WORD LIST				
amoeba	artery	atom	black hole	chlorophyll
constellation	cumulus	herbivore	kelp	magma
monsoon	nectar	ore	precipitation	
protozoa	stalactite	supernova	primate	

SPACE	WEATHER	GEOLOGY

ANIMAL LIFE	PLANT LIFE	MICROSCOPIC WORLD

Date _____

Name _____

A Happy Marriage

When you marry or join two different words you create a new word called a "compound word." Look at the list below. Can you figure out the word that can be added to the *end* of each set of words in these examples to make new compound words? Write the word and the compound words it creates in the blanks. The first one is done for you.

1. half, night, over =   *time (halftime, nighttime, overtime)*

2. every, no, some =   _____

3. bed, bath, store =   _____

4. fire, work, birth =   _____

5. soft, kitchen, gift =   _____

6. border, bee, on =   _____

What word can be added to the *beginning* of each set of words in these examples to make new compound words?

1. ball, line, board =   _____

2. proof, color, melon =   _____

3. bread, cut, stop =   _____

4. ground, pen, mate =   _____

5. fish, gaze, struck =   _____

6. stairs, side, beat =   _____

YOUR TURN

Think of one more set of compound words that use the same word either at the beginning or the end as in the examples above.

Date _____

Name _____

Vocabulary

A Word Sandwich

The words in boldface below can be sandwiched between two other words to create new compound words. Choose the correct boldface word for each example and write the compound words it makes on the blanks. Your choice must work as both the ending of the first word and the beginning of the second. We've done one for you.

HINT: Each word in the list is used only once.

crow   ever   water   fire   flower

hand   light   out   over   post   top

1. cook ____book____ mark
   cookbook, bookmark

2. sun _____ pot
   _____

3. scare _____ bar
   _____

4. sleep _____ flow
   _____

5. tree _____ soil
   _____

6. flash _____ house
   _____

7. what _____ green
   _____

8. work _____ side
   _____

9. wild _____ proof
   _____

10. back _____ cuff
    _____

11. goal _____ card
    _____

12. under _____ front
    _____

YOUR TURN

Add two more examples of words that can be made into compound words like the ones above. See whether your classmates can figure out the missing word in between each of your examples.

Date _____

Name _____

Vocabulary

Come Together

Each numbered item below has three words in the top row and four words in the bottom row. Which word from the top group can combine with the other words in the bottom group to make the most compound words? Circle the word, then write the compound words it creates in the blanks at right. Watch out! In some cases, there may be a tie. We've done the first one for you.

1. (HOUSE,) GATE, BEE

   keeper   boat   hive   guest

   housekeeper, houseboat, houseguest
   _____
   _____
   _____

2. LIGHT, HEAVY, OUT

   house   cast   weight   law

   _____
   _____
   _____
   _____
   _____

3. HAIR, LIFE, TOOTH

   guard   cut   brush   style

   _____
   _____
   _____
   _____
   _____

4. SEA, AIR, EARTH

   line   port   quake   plane

   _____
   _____
   _____
   _____

5. HOME, MAIN, TEAM

   page   land   work   stream

   _____
   _____
   _____
   _____
   _____

6. DOWN, OUT, UP

   stairs   town   pour   back

   _____
   _____
   _____
   _____

YOUR TURN

Compound words do not always join the meanings of the two words used—for example, <u>butterfly</u>. Find another example of a compound word which does not join the meanings of its two words.

FAST FINISHERS

Date _____

Name _____

Animals in Action

When you hear the word *dog*, what do you think of?
No doubt, you think of a fun, furry house pet. But the word
dog also has another meaning besides the animal definition,
which is a noun. When the word acts as a verb, it means
to follow closely. There are lots of animal words that do
double duty this way. Look at the words listed below. Write the letters
of the word's two definitions in the blanks provided.

WORD	MEANING
1. duck _____, _____	**a.** to bother
	b. to close
2. seal _____, _____	**c.** bird of prey
	d. burrowing mammal
3. ram _____, _____	**e.** to mimic
	f. to lower one's head
4. badger _____, _____	**g.** to strike
	h. a small, flying mammal
5. hawk _____, _____	**i.** aquatic bird
	j. male sheep
6. ape _____, _____	**k.** marine mammal
	l. to sell
7. crane _____, _____	**m.** to eat quickly
	n. a wading bird
8. bat _____, _____	**o.** to support or carry
	p. a wild mammal related to dog
9. bear _____, _____	**q.** large carnivorous mammal
	r. gorilla
10. wolf _____, _____	**s.** to hit a ball with a stick
	t. to tilt one's neck

YOUR TURN

Write a paragraph using three of the animal/verb words above.

Date _____

Name _____

A Perfect Match?

Each word in column 1 has a match in column 2.
The match in column 2 is either a synonym (means
the same thing, such as *right* and *correct*), antonym
(means the opposite, such as *right* and *wrong*), or homophone (sounds
the same, such as *one* and *won*). Draw a line between each match and
write which type of match it is. There is only one correct match for
each word.

COLUMN 1	COLUMN 2	TYPE OF MATCH
1. modern	a. where	1. _____
2. sail	b. dusk	2. _____
3. thaw	c. gargantuan	3. _____
4. tired	d. late	4. _____
5. blue	e. sale	5. _____
6. dawn	f. ancient	6. _____
7. right	g. exhausted	7. _____
8. miniscule	h. blew	8. _____
9. wear	j. correct	9. _____
10. tardy	k. freeze	10. _____
11. grate	l. kernel	11. _____
12. assemble	m. live	12. _____
13. danger	n. hazard	13. _____
14. dwell	o. dismantle	14. _____
15. colonel	p. great	15. _____

YOUR TURN

Make a puzzle of your own like the one above. Use synonyms, antonyms,
and homonyms. Then have a classmate figure out what the matches are.

FAST FINISHERS

Vocabulary

Date _____

Name _____

I Ate Eight!

A homophone is a word that has the same sound and perhaps even the same spelling as another word, but a different meaning. For example, *ate* and *eight* are homophones. In each row, write the homophone for each word in the blank next to it. Circle the one word in the group that *doesn't* have a homophone. Abbreviations, contractions, and proper nouns do not count as homophones!

1. peace/_____   site/_____   pail/_____   stay/_____

2. show/_____   board/_____   sent/_____   berry/_____

3. tide/_____   road/_____   roam/_____   seen/_____

4. wade/_____   wick/_____   missed/_____   steel/_____

5. raise/_____   principal/_____   rose/_____   eraser/_____

6. door/_____   fir/_____   titan/_____   prays/_____

7. aisle/_____   towed/_____   claws/_____   rodeo/_____

8. fern/_____   grate/_____   earn/_____   bail/_____

9. thrown/_____   rye/_____   flu/_____   pencil/_____

10. idle/_____   trick/_____   censor/_____   tour/_____

YOUR TURN

Pick three homophones from the exercise above. Write each word and its definition.

_____   _____

_____   _____

_____   _____

Date _____

Name _____

Vocabulary

Opposite and the Same

Circle any word in column 1 that is *both* an antonym *and* a homophone of any word in column 2 and draw two lines to show its matches. For example, the antonym of the word *night* is *day*. The homophone of the word *night* is *knight*. Some words won't have an antonym or a homophone.

COLUMN 1	COLUMN 2
buy	piece
go	strong
new	push
know	sell
mail	clothes
down	short
weak	cold
pull	by
poor	come
full	pour
close	knew
tall	rich
young	open
cold	male
flower	war
peace	week
	old
	flour

YOUR TURN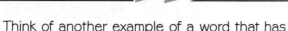

Think of another example of a word that has both an antonym and a homophone like those found in the list above.

FAST FINISHERS

Vocabulary

Date _____

Name _____

Animal Partners

Match each animal with its female and male counterparts by writing the animal's number next to each gender. If you don't know, make your best guess then check a reference source such as a dictionary or the Internet. We've done the first one for you.

HINT: Some male and female animal names are also the names of an entirely different animal.

ANIMAL	FEMALE	MALE
1. deer	cow	billy
2. bee	duck	drone
3. pig	nanny	gander
4. chicken	goose	bull
5. elephant	doe *1*	lion
6. sheep	she-chuck	he-chuck
7. lion	sow	stallion
8. duck	vixen	drake
9. woodchuck	hen	rooster
10. zebra	ewe	boar
11. goose	queen	buck *1*
12. fox	mare	ram
13. goat	lioness	dog

Date _____

Name _____

Good or Great

A *denotation* is the dictionary definition for a word. A *connotation* is the feeling that the word brings to mind in addition to its definition. Below are two lists of words. Look at the words in column 1 and match them with a word in column 2 that means almost the same thing, but with impact. We've done the first one for you. There is only one correct match for each.

COLUMN 1	COLUMN 2	CORRECT MATCH
1. closing	**a.** shove	*1. k*
2. filled	**b.** weird	_____
3. took	**c.** run-down	_____
4. walked	**d.** dragged	_____
5. broke up with	**e.** hilarious	_____
6. clapped	**f.** cheered	_____
7. small	**g.** great	_____
8. interested	**h.** chug	_____
9. funny	**i.** harmony	_____
10. good	**j.** tiny	_____
11. push	**k.** slamming	_____
12. droopy	**l.** snatched	_____
13. sip	**m.** fascinated	_____
14. unusual	**n.** flooded	_____
15. escorted	**o.** stomped	_____
16. agreement	**p.** dumped	_____

YOUR TURN

Look at the connotation of each word listed in column 2. Which connotations are positive? Which are negative?

Date _____

Name _____

FAST FINISHERS

Vocabulary

Deeply Rooted

Below is a series of Latin and Greek roots that appear in modern English. Latin roots are indicated with an "L" and Greek roots with "G." Write three words using each root for each example. Then use the words you created to guess at the meaning of the root in the space provided. We've done the first one for you.

A. VISI (L) ⟹ Meaning: _____ *See* _____

1. _*Visible*_   2. _*Vision*_   3. _*Visit*_

B. AUD (L) ⟹ Meaning: _____

1. _____   2. _____   3. _____

C. GRAPH (G) ⟹ Meaning: _____

1. _____   2. _____   3. _____

D. DUC (L) ⟹ Meaning: _____

1. _____   2. _____   3. _____

E. PHON (G) ⟹ Meaning: _____

1. _____   2. _____   3. _____

F. GRAM (G) ⟹ Meaning: _____

1. _____   2. _____   3. _____

YOUR TURN

Choose a word from the list above and use it in a sentence to show that you understand its meaning.

_____

_____

_____

Date _____

Name _____

Vocabulary

All in the Family

Word families are groups of words that are related in two ways: They have the same root or base word and they have similar meanings. For example, in Latin *pop* means *people*. So the meanings of all the words in this word family—*population, popular, populace*—all have to do with people. Below are some words from three more word families. Draw a line to match the words in each family with their meanings. Then underline the base word that appears in each word. If you need help, use the sentences below each word-family list. They will give you context clues to the words' meanings.

WORD FAMILY 1   **MEANINGS**

manual   to handle
manipulate   a book or paper often written by hand
manuscript   done by the hands; related to the hands

   The magician wrote a *manuscript* **about how it takes great** *manual* **ability to** *manipulate* **magic equipment properly.**

WORD FAMILY 2   **MEANINGS**

peddle   someone going on foot
pedicure   to travel around selling something, usually on foot
pedestrian   care of the feet, toes, and nails

   After the salesperson had *peddled* **all her products to** *pedestrians* **walking by, she went home and gave herself a** *pedicure*.

WORD FAMILY 3   **MEANINGS**

vital   energy or liveliness
vitality   full of life and energy; important
vitamin   a substance needed by the body for a healthful life

   In order for people to have *vitality*, **it is** *vital* **that they exercise and take the right** *vitamins* **every day.**

YOUR TURN

Look at the three roots you underlined for each word family. Take a guess at each of their meanings based on each word's definition.

_____   _____

_____   _____

_____   _____

Date _____

Name _____

Vocabulary

More or Less?

Each pair of words in bold below are followed
by a list of seven words. Test each of those seven
words to see if they can form a new word with either
or both of the words in the pair above them. Write the
correct compound word for each, or write "neither" if a
compound word can't be created. We've done the first
one for you.

"MORE" OR "LESS"

1. end _endless_

2. any _____

3. over _____

4. many _____

5. use _____

6. ever _____

7. some _____

> **HINT:** In some cases, more than one word can be created.

"IN" OR "OUT"

1. side _____

2. with _____

3. cut _____

4. board _____

5. root _____

6. cast _____

7. land _____

"UNDER" OR "OVER"

1. ground _____

2. go _____

3. more _____

4. hear _____

5. roll _____

6. place _____

7. stood _____

Date _____

Name _____

Vocabulary

Big or Bird?

Are the following words listed below synonyms for *big* or are they types of birds? Circle the correct choice. Guess first if you don't know, then use a reference source to help you.

WORD LIST

1.	BIG	⟸	mammoth ⟹	BIRD
2.	BIG	⟸	bullfinch ⟹	BIRD
3.	BIG	⟸	ibis ⟹	BIRD
4.	BIG	⟸	gargantuan ⟹	BIRD
5.	BIG	⟸	colossal ⟹	BIRD
6.	BIG	⟸	hulking ⟹	BIRD
7.	BIG	⟸	egret ⟹	BIRD
8.	BIG	⟸	vast ⟹	BIRD
9.	BIG	⟸	mallard ⟹	BIRD
10.	BIG	⟸	thrush ⟹	BIRD
11.	BIG	⟸	hefty ⟹	BIRD
12.	BIG	⟸	grouse ⟹	BIRD
13.	BIG	⟸	peregrine ⟹	BIRD

FAST FINISHERS

Vocabulary

Date _____

Name _____

Word Works

Each letter or group of letters is missing either the prefix "ex-," or "com-," or the suffix "-ence," or "-ic" to make it a real word. Your job is to figure out which prefix or suffix works best. Write the word formed and its meaning in the space provided. There is only one correct answer for each. You may use a dictionary to check your answers.

Examples:
bat ➜ adding "com-" to the front makes it "combat"
histor ➜ adding "-ic" at the end makes it "historic"

LETTERS	EX-, COM-, -ENCE, OR -IC?	WORD FORMED	MEANING?
1. fort			
2. poet			
3. viol			
4. it			
5. publ			
6. bine			
7. abs			
8. haust			
9. ceed			

YOUR TURN

Look at the words formed and their definitions above, then take a guess at the meanings of the suffixes or prefixes used with them. Use a dictionary to check your guess.

ex- _____

com- _____

-ence _____

-ic _____

Date _____

Name _____

Vocabulary

ZIP It

A ZIP code: Everyone in the United States has one, but not everyone knows what the abbreviation "ZIP" stands for. Cross out the contents of this grid as instructed below including repeats. The letters that remain will give you the answer!

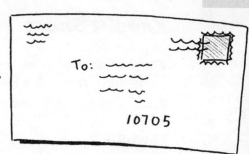

f	w	q	z	h	s
o	b	n	y	u	e
u	x	b	d	h	y
x	k	f	c	i	u
s	m	p	j	b	r
c	s	h	o	w	v
u	e	s	m	y	e
f	k	n	x	t	p
f	d	l	b	q	s
a	j	n	w	f	u

WHAT TO CROSS OUT

- All consonants in "quick"
- The sixth consonant in the alphabet
- The one letter found in all of these words: way, awe, wee
- The letter that would make "bear" plural
- Any consonants between (but not including) "c" and "g"
- The vowel that rhymes with "2"
- Any consonant that rhymes with "k"
- The consonant that sounds the same as the name of an insect
- The third-to-last consonant
- Any consonant that rhymes with "i"

THE ANSWER

Write the remaining letters from the grid in order and you should see the answer more clearly.

HINT: You may want to group the letters into words first!

ZIP = _____

_____

Date _____

Name _____

FAST FINISHERS

Vocabulary

Keep It Short

Which of these words have common abbreviations that are also words?
Circle them. Guess first if you don't know, but you may use a reference source
if you're really stuck. We've done the first one for you.

WORD	ABBREVIATION	IS IT A WORD?
(1. patent ➔)	*pat.*	☒ yes ☐ no
2. street ➔	_____	☐ yes ☐ no
3. apartment ➔	_____	☐ yes ☐ no
4. Wednesday ➔	_____	☐ yes ☐ no
5. boulevard ➔	_____	☐ yes ☐ no
6. officer ➔	_____	☐ yes ☐ no
7. continued ➔	_____	☐ yes ☐ no
8. attention ➔	_____	☐ yes ☐ no
9. government ➔	_____	☐ yes ☐ no
10. producer ➔	_____	☐ yes ☐ no
11. singular ➔	_____	☐ yes ☐ no
12. literature ➔	_____	☐ yes ☐ no
13. doctor ➔	_____	☐ yes ☐ no
14. Maine ➔	_____	☐ yes ☐ no
15. Reverend ➔	_____	☐ yes ☐ no

YOUR TURN

Think of three more words and their abbreviations. Then ask a classmate
to identify those, if any, that are also a word(s) in their abbreviated forms.

_____ ➔ _____		☐ yes ☐ no
_____ ➔ _____		☐ yes ☐ no
_____ ➔ _____		☐ yes ☐ no

Date _____

Name _____

Acronym or Not?

ZIP (as in "ZIP code") is an acronym that stands for "**Z**one **I**mprovement **P**lan." Below is a list of common words, some of which are also acronyms. Circle the acronyms—even if you're not sure what they stand for. Then write out what you think each letter stands for. If you don't know, guess! Then you may use a reference source to see whether you were correct. We've done the first one for you.

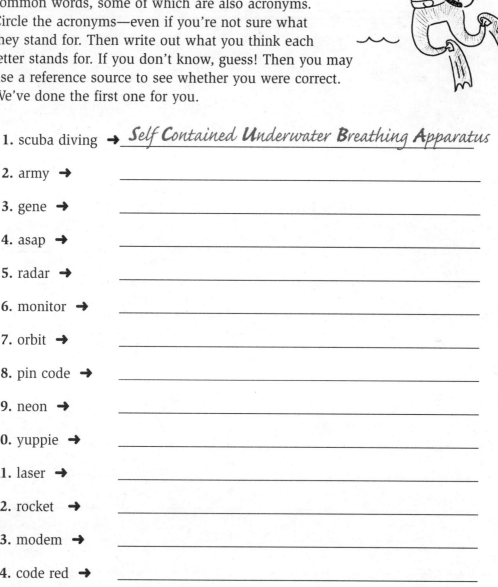

1. scuba diving → _Self Contained Underwater Breathing Apparatus_

2. army → _____

3. gene → _____

4. asap → _____

5. radar → _____

6. monitor → _____

7. orbit → _____

8. pin code → _____

9. neon → _____

10. yuppie → _____

11. laser → _____

12. rocket → _____

13. modem → _____

14. code red → _____

15. artery → _____

16. swat → _____

Date _____

Name _____

Vocabulary

Collecting Compounds

Look at the list of words in the box below. How many compound words can you make from these twelve words? Write as many as you can in the blanks.

WORD LIST			
light	back	life	house
time	fire	flash	board
man	head	night	out

COMPOUND WORDS THAT CAN BE CREATED

_____   _____

_____   _____

_____   _____

_____   _____

_____   _____

_____   _____

_____   _____

_____   _____

_____   _____

_____   _____

_____   _____

_____   _____

Date _____

Name _____

Vocabulary

All About Analogies

What do a mermaid and a centaur have to do with each other? Below is a series of analogies. Solve each one. The number of blanks for each analogy will give you a clue as to how many letters each missing word has. We've done the first one for you.

1. **mermaid** is to **fish** as **centaur** is to _h o r s e_

2. **green** is to __ __ as **red** is to **stop**

3. **ask** is to **asked** as **tell** is to __ __ __ __

4. __ __ __ is to **finger** as **foot** is to **hand**

5. **fork** is to **spaghetti** as __ __ __ __ __ __ is to **yogurt**

6. **orange** is to **grove** as **apple** is to __ __ __ __ __ __ __ __

7. **Topeka** is to **Kansas** as **Tokyo** is to __ __ __ __ __ __

8. **bee** is to __ __ __ __ as **wasp** is to **nest**

9. **row** is to **horizontal** as __ __ __ __ __ __ __ is to **vertical**

10. **moon** is to **Earth** as **Earth** is to __ __ __

11. __ __ __ __ __ __ is to **quiver** as **sword** is to **sheath**

> A mermaid is a mythical creature with a human upper body and a fish lower body. A centaur is a mythical creature with a human upper body and a horse lower body. As a result, mermaid is to fish as centaur is to horse.

BONUS ANALOGY

yolk **is to** egg **as** eye **is to** | e a n h i c u r r |

> To figure out the answer, you'll need to unscramble the letters in the box!

Answer: __ __ __ __ __ __ __ __ __

Date _____

Name _____

FAST FINISHERS

Vocabulary

One Word, Two Meanings

Each sentence has two blanks, which can be filled with one word
that has multiple meanings. Use clues in the sentences to figure out and test
the correct missing word. Then, fill in the blanks. We've done one for you.

1. Sally ___*left*___ her umbrella on the floor of the closet, to the
   ___*left*___ of the vacuum cleaner.

2. I dropped my buttered _____ under the table and heard it
   _____ across the floor.

3. After Kurt broke his leg, the entire _____ of the play signed
   his _____.

4. Before we watch the _____, I will _____ you the
   theater where it is running.

5. After we chose a nice _____ for our picnic, I noticed a _____
   on my shirt.

6. The _____ in her backyard is over 100 years old, but it has aged
   very _____.

7. It will _____ my spirits if I get a _____ at work.

8. I am a _____ of opening the window to get fresh air, but I'll also
   use a _____ if it's too hot.

9. The forest ranger could not _____ to see the _____ caught in
   a trap.

10. She will _____ in a movie about an astronomer who discovers
    a new nearby _____.

11. For Mary, it was a total _____ to catch a _____ during the
    camping trip since they don't normally swim where she was fishing.

12. I _____ the gauze tightly around the _____ so it wouldn't
    bleed or get infected.

Date _____

Name _____

E-mail Order

You've just gotten a new job at a marketing company and your first assignment is to alphabetize these e-mail addresses. Trouble is, the computers are down, so you need to do it with the computer in your head! To get the job done right, you'll need to remember to alphabetize letters first, then numbers. Place the addresses in the correct order in the blanks provided.

E-MAIL ADDRESSES	CORRECT ALPHABETICAL ORDER
mm01@cyberama.com	_____
mon02@cyberinc.com	_____
moo01@cyberocity.com	_____
mm12@cyberspaceship.com	_____
mnm1@cyberstorm.com	_____
mnn02@cybercafe.com	_____
m10@cyberplanet.com	_____
mm12@cyberscape.com	_____
moo1@cybersimple.com	_____
mmm123@cybertek.com	_____
mz@cyberfuse.com	_____
moo1@cybershow.com	_____
mnm1@cyberquak.com	_____
mm01@cyberzoo.com	_____
mmm1234@cybertek.com	_____

YOUR TURN

Create a list of Web addresses using the ones above as a model. Have your classmates sort them in alphabetical order.

FAST FINISHERS

Vocabulary

Date _____

Name _____

Alphabetical Anarchy

The words below are alphabetized—but not by their first letters. Write what letter (2nd, 3rd, etc.) determines the alphabetical order for each example. We've done the first one for you.

1. Saturday, Wednesday, Thursday, Monday, Friday, Tuesday, Sunday
The 2nd letter in each word determines this alphabetical order.

2. drawbridge, escapade, plentiful, combustion, menagerie

_____

3. kindergarten, avalanche, cornucopia, thesaurus, labyrinth

_____

4. swashbuckler, biodegradable, whimsical, turbulence, potpourri

_____

5. hippopotamus, stratosphere, mesmerizing, cantaloupe, exaggerate

_____

6. fallacious, vestibule, pneumatic, oxymoron, epigraph

_____

7. pessimistic, metamorphic, tiresome, unadulterated, vociferous

_____

8. commiserate, attainment, versatile, quagmire, humanitarian

_____

9. plethora, pandemonium, pensive, problematic, procrastinate

_____

10. absentia, confused, diatribe, synchronize, xylophone

_____

YOUR TURN

Write down four words that all contain six letters, then alphabetize them by their second-to-last letters.

_____   _____   _____   _____

_____   _____   _____   _____

54

Date _____

Name _____

Vocabulary

Pages From the Dictionary

Most dictionaries list two guide words at the top of each page: the first and last entries on that page. If you saw the words "**camel** *to* **candle**" at the top of the page, you would find all the words between those two entries in alphabetical order. Below are boldface pairs of guide words like those you might find at the top of a dictionary page. One word on each list would not appear on the page indicated by the two words given. Circle that word. We've done the first one for you.

"Blot" would not be on the page that begins with "blouse" and ends with "blunt."

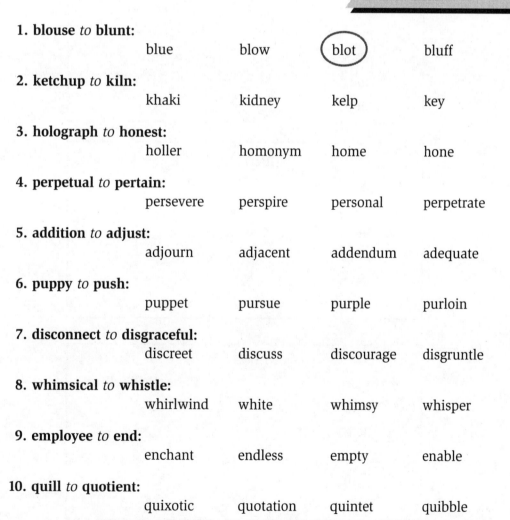

1. **blouse** *to* **blunt:**

   blue   blow   ⟨blot⟩   bluff

2. **ketchup** *to* **kiln:**

   khaki   kidney   kelp   key

3. **holograph** *to* **honest:**

   holler   homonym   home   hone

4. **perpetual** *to* **pertain:**

   persevere   perspire   personal   perpetrate

5. **addition** *to* **adjust:**

   adjourn   adjacent   addendum   adequate

6. **puppy** *to* **push:**

   puppet   pursue   purple   purloin

7. **disconnect** *to* **disgraceful:**

   discreet   discuss   discourage   disgruntle

8. **whimsical** *to* **whistle:**

   whirlwind   white   whimsy   whisper

9. **employee** *to* **end:**

   enchant   endless   empty   enable

10. **quill** *to* **quotient:**

    quixotic   quotation   quintet   quibble

Date _____

Name _____

FAST FINISHERS

Vocabulary

Fun With Fə net′iks

Words don't always spell out the way they sound. If you don't know how to pronounce a word, you can always look it up in a dictionary and see its phonetic spelling there. The phonetic spelling of a word shows how it is pronounced. Below is a series of grids with words and their phonetic spellings. Match the correct pairs by drawing a line from the word in the left column to its correct phonetic spelling in the right column. If you don't know what some of the symbols mean, use a dictionary or other reference source to help you.

GRID 1

Word	Phonetic Spelling
phony	fīn
phone	fan
fan	fun′ē
fine	fō′nē
funny	fōn

GRID 2

Word	Phonetic Spelling
story	stär′ē
stir	stôr′ē
store	stär
starry	stûr
stare	stôr′

GRID 3

Word	Phonetic Spelling
herb	hâr
hair	hī ə r
hire	hēr′ō
hero	hâr′ē
hairy	ûrb

FAST FINISHERS

Vocabulary

Date _____

Name _____

Dots in the Wrong Place

As in the dictionary, each of these words is broken into syllables. But beware! One dot—otherwise known as a syllable break—is in the wrong place. Write each word with the correct syllable break in the blanks. Guess if you don't know, then check a dictionary for the answer.

1. as·se·mbly   _____

2. aud·i·to·ri·um   _____

3. caf·et·e·ri·a   _____

4. el·e·ment·a·ry   _____

5. ex·am·i·nati·on   _____

6. gra·du·a·tion   _____

7. gym·na·s·ium   _____

8. prin·cip·al   _____

9. el·im·i·nate   _____

10. hi·er·o·gly·phics _____

11. pe·dia·tri·cian   _____

12. cho·re·og·raph·er _____

13. re·con·si·der   _____

14. met·am·or·phic   _____

15. sop·his·ti·ca·ted _____

YOUR TURN

Write five words broken into syllables. Make sure one syllable break in each word is incorrect. Then have your classmates write each word with the correct syllabication.

FAST FINISHERS

Vocabulary

Date _____

Name _____

Syllable Wizardry

How good are you at building words and figuring out how many syllables they have? Answer these tricky and fun questions about words to find out. Some questions may have more than one answer. Write your answers in the blanks.

TIPS
- No answers are proper nouns.
- No answers are foreign words.
- Do not rearrange or subtract any letters from the given word to form the new word.

1. What letter can you add to "eve" to make it a common *two*-syllable word?

Letter _____ New word _____

2. What letter can you add to "sleep" to make it a common *two*-syllable word?

Letter _____ New word _____

3. What letter can you add to "rise" to make it a common *two*-syllable word?

Letter _____ New word _____

4. What letter can you add to "rode" to make it a common *two*-syllable word?

Letter _____ New word _____

5. What letter can you add to "rode" to make it a common *three*-syllable word?

Letter _____ New word _____

6. What letter can you add to "man" to make it a common *two*-syllable word?

Letter _____ New word _____

7. What letter can you add to "are" to make it a common *three*-syllable word?

Letter _____ New word _____

8. What letter can you add to "pen" to make it a common *two*-syllable word?

Letter _____ New word _____

9. What letter can you add to "came" to make it a common *two*-syllable word?

Letter _____ New word _____

10. What letter can you add to "came" to make it a common *three*-syllable word?

Letter _____ New word _____

FAST FINISHERS

Vocabulary

Alphabet Soup

Look at the symbols and numbers listed below. Use words to spell out each one, then alphabetize this list of symbols and numbers based on the letters they contain.

SYMBOL/ NUMBER	SYMBOL/NUMBER SPELLED OUT	CORRECT ALPHABETICAL ORDER
1. 36	_____	_____
2. ?	_____	_____
3. ;	_____	_____
4. *	_____	_____
5. (	_____	_____
6. 0	_____	_____
7. [	_____	_____
8. '	_____	_____
9. 258	_____	_____
10. &	_____	_____
11. 789	_____	_____
12. "	_____	_____

FAST FINISHERS

Date _____

Name _____

Vocabulary

First Words

Sometimes words cannot be traced to a specific year of origin, but most can be traced to a certain period of time. With that in mind, guess which word in each pair came into use in the English language first. Circle it. Then explain your choice in the blank provided. There is only one correct answer for each. When done, read about these words' origins in a dictionary.

1.   oven   refrigerator

_____

2.   airplane   bicycle

_____

3.   clock   wristwatch

_____

4.   dinosaur   monkey

_____

5.   snowball   snowman

_____

6.   genetics   fingerprinting

_____

7.   adobe   plywood

_____

8.   noun   adverb

_____

9.   poem   song

_____

10.   sorceress   wizard

_____

11.   baseball   soccer

_____

12.   black   blue

_____

ANSWERS

Page 6: Not Your Usual Crossword
Across: 5. sphere (orb) 7. to prevent something (foil) 8. mythical creature (elf) 10. not take part in (exempt)
Down: 2. hot breakfast (oatmeal) 3. a group of three (trio) 4. regular (normal) 6. a secret plan (plot) 9. transmit document by phone line (fax)

Page 7: Can You Smell a Rat?
The following words aren't real:
1. polkera 2. kloogus 3. Scotzygan 4. gundeel 5. siltic 6. rodotephobia

Page 8: The One Word
Center column spells somnambulist: sheets, snooze, dream, snore, nap, pajamas, blanket, shuteye, pillow, midnight, sleepy, bedtime
A somnambulist is a person who walks in his sleep.

Page 9: You're Breaking Up
Smaller words are as follows:
1. robe/doll 2. pail/near 3. ghost/mine 4. wasp/rods 5. tour/stub 6. sew/theater 7. bust/rout 8. snake/flow.

Page 10: The Name Game
2. Velocity 3000 3. Provincial Travel 4. *Jester's Handbook* 5. Tranquility Inn 6. Etiquette 7. Mosaic 8. Resonate Hall 9. Luminous Gel 10. Microscopasaurus

Page 11: Jumbled and Incomplete
2. d – dream, drizzle, distant
3. o – globe, rainbow, journey
4. b – beach, brave, boring
5. i – milk, winter, bicycle
6. c – comet, carrot, creature
7. j – joke, jungle, juggle
8. w – crow, answer, whisper

Page 12: Rhyme With Reason
1.d, z – doze 2. g, p – grape 3. b, d, g, d – bodyguard 4. b, z – blaze 5. v, g, t, b – vegetable 6. v, d – invade 7. t, g, t – target 8. d, v, c – advice 9. g , z – gauze 10. d, p, t – depart

Page 13: Fall Back or Spring Ahead?
2. stalactite 3. feeble 4. hemisphere 5. transparent 6. accomplice 7. brine 8. a cappella 9. diminutive 10. duckbill

Page 14: Letters on the Run
1. oasis 2. eerie 3. icicle 4. rewind 5. orchard 6. protect 7. hammock 8. envelope

Page 15: EE-ther OAr
3. no (feet yes, foat no) 4. no (meen no, moan yes) 5. yes (seer and soar) 6. yes (fleet and float) 7. yes (meet and moat) 8. no (seed yes, soad no) 9. no (sleet yes, sloat no) 10. yes (beet and boat) 11. no (reer no, roar yes) 12. no (teer and toar) 13. yes (seek and soak) 14. no (peek yes, poak no) 15. yes (creek and croak)

Page 16: Four Squares
Grid 1: jackal, koala, llama, muskrat; should *not* be circled: eel, lobster, snake, wasp
Grid 2: chapter, page, preface, spine; should *not* be circled: bookmark, library, shelf
Grid 3: Bolivia, Chile, Ecuador, Uruguay; should *not* be circled: Cuba, France, India
Grid 4: emerald, jade, kelly, olive; should *not* be circled: crimson, ebony

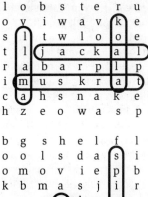

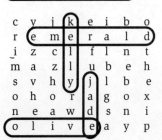

Page 17: Out Of Here!
2. pavement (9 / weapons) 3. palette (8 / bodies of water) 4. bog (7 / communities) 5. creek (3 / big cats) 6. triathlon (10 / three-dimensional objects) 7. puma (5 / wet areas of land) 8. catapult (2 / painting terms) 9. hamlet (4 / road surfaces) 10. shin (1 / track and field events)

Page 18: Say What?
Correct answers from word find are as follows with dummy answers in parentheses:
1. fourteen (twelve, forty) 2. clavicle (femur, sternum) 3. brackets (parentheses) 4. bovine (canine, ursine) 5. czar (king, pharaoh) 6. typhoon (tornado, whirlpool) 7. spiders (heights, dark) 8. thrice (no dummy answers)

WORD FIND

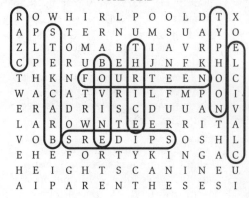

Page 19: Change Is in the Air
2. house 3. noon; 4. dinner 5. sideways 6. smashed 7. window 8. book 9. people 10. strange 11. pen 12. reward.

Page 20: Definition Plugs
2. language 3. symphony 4. ground 5. produce 6. instrument 7. pencil 8. seize 9. period 10. grammar 11. young 12. grasp 13. farm 14. orchestra 15. music

Page 21: E-ttachments

H (Jan.)

Sorry it took me so long to write back. My family just got back from a trip to Lake Erie. We rode through New York, Pennsylvania, and Ohio and ended up in the great state of Michigan. My parents have been there in the past but my sister and I never have. One of the most spectacular things we saw was a huge migration of birds over the water. We stayed up late the whole week. The sky was so clear you could see a star in any direction. It could get very cold, worse than sitting next to an air conditioner vent. Sometimes we would sit on a bench at the shore and hug each other to stay warm! Once we saw some motion in the water and thought we saw the fin of some large animal, but it was just a breeze blowing over the surface. It was dusk and the daylight was so dim that you couldn't blame us for it! It was nice to be someplace where you can hear gentle waves lapping all night. There were a ton of people on vacation there, though the crowd included a whole unit of police officers. They were having some kind of conference. I stood next to one of them in line at the buffet and she asked if I was having a good time. Of course, I said yes. She looked at my plate of food and quipped, "I knew you'd say that—I've never seen so much food on such a small plate. Where does a small bony person like you fit all of that food?" I laughed so much that I dropped my fork, and it rang when it hit the floor. I must have looked so clumsy to her.

You should definitely go sometime!

Your friend,
Tim

Jan (Jane); to (toe); trip (tripe); Erie (eerie); we (ewe and wee); rode (erode); the (thee); state (estate); past (paste); migration (emigration); late (elate); star (stare); very (every); than (Ethan); vent (event); sit (site); on (one); at (ate and eat); hug (huge); motion (emotion); fin (fine); dim (dime); us (use); for (fore); be (bee); can (cane); ton (tone); unit (unite); yes (eyes); quipped (equipped); bony (ebony); rang (range); her (here); go (ego); Tim (time)

Page 22: One Word, Two Words
2. light (luminous, spectrum), house (abode, domicile) 3. gold (bullion, karat), fish (cod, grouper) 4. flower (orchid, geranium), pot (cauldron, wok) 5. bed (trundle, futon), rock (slate, obsidian) 6. red (crimson, rouge), head (cranium, noggin) 7. play (frolic, romp), mate (partner, associate) 8. under (beneath, underneath), take (get, secure)

Page 23: Inside Information
2. g (coin/fountain) 3. h (pupil/eye) 4. f (pig/sty) 5. a (helium/balloon) 6. b (cereal/ pantry) 7. c (assets/ vault) 8. d (rake/shed) 9. n (license/ wallet) 10. l (arrow/quiver) 11. k (battery/flashlight) 12. m (mercury/thermometer) 13. j (lint/dryer) 14. o (reflection/ mirror) 15. i (message/bottle)

Page 24: Double the Fun
2. yes 3. no; spelling wrong; Egypt 4. yes 5. no; spelling wrong; Mississippi 6. no; both wrong; Everest is highest mountain; correct spelling is Kilimanjaro 7. no; spelling wrong; Juneau (Alaska) 8. no; geography wrong; Beijing 9. yes 10. no; geography wrong; Northern Ireland

Page 25: It All Adds Up
1. meter 2. decimal point 3. Celsius 4. seventy-five 5. octagon 6. thousand

I	C	T	D	M	O	E	I	I	T
P	V	U	E	E	S	F	M	L	C
C	T	N	N	T	N	T	D	E	O
E	G	V	N	O	E	E	R	A	T
E	A	H	S	A	A	S	B	R	H
L	Y	U	I	S	D	N	U	O	S

Mystery Question
What is a number that is subtracted from another number called?
Answer: Subtrahend

Page 26: Blue Moon
1. blue 2. moon (Jupiter) 3. moon (Mars) 4. blue; 5. blue 6. moon (Pluto) 7. blue; 8. blue 9. moon (Uranus) 10. moon (Saturn)

Page 27: The Class Is All Ears
1. feet 2. tongue 3. brain or liver 4. ears 5. eyes 6. heart 7. lungs 8. teeth

Page 28: State of the Art
1. Kentucky, New Jersey 2. Delaware, Florida, Georgia, Hawaii, Louisiana, Pennsylvania, Rhode Island, Utah 3. Ohio, Iowa, Maine 4. Alabama, Alaska, Arizona 5. Arkansas (Kansas), West Virginia (Virginia) 6. Idaho, Indiana, Iowa, Oklahoma 7. Hawaii, Idaho, Maine, Utah 8. Georgia, Kansas, New York, Texas, Utah, Vermont 9. Connecticut, Illinois, Massachusetts, Minnesota, Mississippi, Missouri, Pennsylvania, Tennessee 10. Florida, Rhode Island, Wyoming 11. Nebraska, Nevada, North Carolina, North Dakota 12. Hawaii, Tennessee

Page 29: All Mixed Up
(Chart 1) Category 1: Outside the body – thumbnail, eyelash, scalp, temple; Category 2: Inside the body – capillary, esophagus (Chart 2) Category 1 – U.S. Presidents: Jefferson (Thomas), Reagan (Ronald), Wilson (Woodrow); Category 2 – Famous Inventors: Edison (Thomas), Carver (George Washington), Wright (Orville) (Chart 3) Category 1 – Valleys: canyon, gorge, ravine; Category 2 – Peaks: mountain, hilltop, crest

Page 30: Earth, Wind, and Fire
1. topsoil (earth) 2. inferno (fire) 3. tide (water) 4. cultivate (earth) 5. cloud (air or water) 6. combustible (fire) 7. dew (water) 8. oxygen (air or fire) 9. atmosphere (air) 10. ember (fire) 11. condensation (water) 12. arid (earth) 13. altitude (air) 14. molten (fire) 15. crust (earth)

Page 31: From This to That
1. Words should be in order from the *smallest in area* to the *biggest in area* as follows: town, city, county, continent, hemisphere
2. Words should be in order from *earliest time period* to *most recent time period* as follows: Neanderthal, Roman Gladiator, Viking, medieval knight, Pilgrim
3. Words should be in order from *least in amount* to *greatest in amount* as follows: dozen, score, gross, million, billion

Page 32: Amazing Science
space: black hole, constellation, supernova; *weather:* monsoon, precipitation, cumulus; *geology:* stalactite, magma, ore; *animal life:* herbivore*, primate, artery; *plant life:* kelp, nectar, chlorophyll; *microscopic world* atom, amoeba, protozoa
If students have different answers, have them explain why. For example, a herbivore* is an animal that eats plants, so this word could also be under plant life.

Page 33: A Happy Marriage
Word that can be attached to the *end:*
2. thing (everything, nothing, something) 3. room (bedroom, bathroom, storeroom) 4. place (fireplace, workplace, birthplace) 5. ware (software, kitchenware, giftware) 6. line (borderline, beeline, online)
Word that can be attached to the *beginning:*
1. base (baseball, baseline, baseboard) 2. water (waterproof, watercolor, watermelon) 3. short (shortbread, shortcut, shortstop) 4. play (playground, playpen, playmate)
5. star (starfish, stargaze, starstruck)
6. up *or* down (upstairs/downstairs, upside/downside, upbeat/downbeat)

Page 34: A Word Sandwich
2. flower (sunflower, flowerpot)
3. crow (scarecrow, crowbar)
4. over (sleepover, overflow)
5. top (treetop, topsoil)
6. light (flashlight, lighthouse)
7. ever (whatever, evergreen)
8. out (workout, outside)
9. fire (wildfire, fireproof)
10. hand (backhand, handcuff)
11. post (goalpost, postcard)
12. water (underwater, waterwheel)

Page 35: Come Together
The following underlined words make the most compound words:
2. out (outhouse, outcast, outlaw). Light only made two words (lighthouse, lightweight) and the word heavy only made one word (heavyweight); 3. hair (haircut, hairbrush, hairstyle). Life only made two words (lifeguard, lifestyle) and the word tooth only made one word (toothbrush).; 4. TIE – sea and air (seaport, seaquake, seaplane; airline, airport, airplane). Earth only made one word (earthquake); 5. home (homepage, homeland, homework). Main only made two words (mainland, mainstream) and team made one word (teamwork); 6. down (downtown, downstairs, downpour. Out made two words (outback, outpour) and up made two words (uptown, upstairs).

Page 36: Animals in Action
The following words should be matched with these two definitions:
1.f, i 2. b, k 3. g, j 4. a, d 5. l, c
6. e, r 7. t, n 8. s, h 9. o, q 10. p, m

Page 37: A Perfect Match?
Words should be matched as follows:
1. f. modern/ancient (antonym) 2. e. sail/sale (homonym) 3. k. thaw/freeze (antonym) 4. g. tired/exhausted (synonym) 5. h. blue/blew (homonym) 6. b. dawn/sunset (antonym) 7. j. right/correct (synonym) 8. c. miniscule/gargantuan (antonym) 9. a. wear/where (homonym) 10. d. tardy/late (synonym) 11. p. grate/great (homonym) 12. o. offer/refuse (antonym) 13. n. danger/hazard (synonym) 14. m. dwell/live (synonym) 15. l. colonel/kernel (homonym)

Page 38: I Ate Eight!
The words in parentheses are homophones; boldface words should be circled:
1. peace (piece); site (sight, cite), pail (pale), **stay** 2. **show**, board (bored), sent (cent, scent), berry (bury) 3. tide (tied), road (rode, rowed), **roam**, seen (scene) 4. wade (weighed), **wick**, missed (mist), steel (steal) 5. raise (rays, raze), principal (principle), rose (rows), **eraser** 6. **door**, fir (fur), titan (tighten), prays (praise) 7. aisle (isle), towed (toad), claws (clause), **rodeo** 8. **fern**, grate (great), bail (bale) 9. thrown (throne), rye (wry); flu (flew, flue); **pencil**; 10. idle (idol), **trick**, earn (urn), tour (tore)

Page 39: Opposite and the Same
buy–sell (antonym), by (homonym); new–old (antonym), knew (homonym); weak–strong (antonym), week (homonym); poor–rich (antonym), pour (homonym); close–open (antonym), clothes (homonym); peace–war (antonym), piece (homonym)

Page 40: Animal Partners
Animal names should be matched by gender as follows (female listed first, male second):
2. bee: queen, drone 3. pig: sow, boar 4. chicken: hen, rooster 5. elephant: cow, bull 6. sheep: ewe, ram 7. lion: lioness, lion 8. duck: duck, drake 9. woodchuck: she-chuck, he-chuck 10. zebra: mare, stallion 11. goose: goose, gander 12. fox: vixen, dog 13. goat: nanny, billy

Page 41: Good or Great
2. n 3. l 4. o 5. p 6. f 7. j 8. m 9. e 10. g 11. a 12. c 13. h 14. b 15. d 16. i
Your Turn: Words that have a positive connotation: cheered, fascinated, hilarious, great, harmony.
Words that have a negative connotation: slammed, flooded, snatched, stomped, dumped, tiny, shove, rundown, seize, weird, dragged

Page 42: Deeply Rooted
B. **aud** ⇨ audience, auditorium, audiovisual, audible, audition **Meaning:** hear C. **graph** ⇨ telegraph, photograph, phonograph, autograph **Meaning:** write D. **duc** ⇨ reduce, conduct, duct **Meaning:** lead E. **phon** ⇨ phonograph, symphony, telephone, microphone, phonics **Meaning:** sound F. **gram** ⇨ telegram, diagram, grammar, epigram, monogram **Meaning:** letter, written

Page 43: All in the Family
Word Family 1 manual (done by the hands; related to the hands); manipulate (to handle well); manuscript (a book or paper often written by hand); Root-*man* which means *hand*.
Word Family 2 peddle (to travel around selling something, usually on foot); pedicure (care of the feet, toes, and nails); pedestrian (someone going on foot); root-*ped* which means *foot*.
Word Family 3 vital (full of life and energy; important); vitality (energy or liveliness); vitamin (a substance needed by the body for a healthful life); Root-*vita* which means *life*

Page 44: More or Less?
Compound words with "more" or "less":
any – anymore; over – moreover; many – neither; use – useless; ever – evermore; some – neither
Compound words with "in" or "out":
side – inside, outside; with – within, without; cut – cutout; board – inboard, outboard; root – neither; cast – outcast; land – inland; outland
Compound words with "under" or "over":
ground – underground, overground; go – undergo; more – moreover; hear – overhear; roll – rollover; place – neither; stood – understood

Page 45: Big or Bird?
1. big 2. bird 3. bird 4. big 5. big 6. big 7. bird 8. big 9. bird 10. bird 11. big 12. bird 13. bird 14. bird

Page 46: Word Works
Words formed and definitions (in parentheses) are as follows:
1. comfort (the feeling of being relaxed and free from pain and worry) 2. poetic (having the qualities of poems) 3. violence (the use of physical force) 4. exit (to leave or go out) 5. public (something that belongs or can be used by everybody) 6. combine (to join or mix two or more things together) 7. absence (the state of being away or not present) 8. exhaust (the waste gases produced by the engine of an automobile) 9. exceed (to be greater or better than something else)
Your Turn: ex – out; com – with; ence – state or quality of; ic – relating to

Page 47: ZIP It

f	w	q	z	h	s
o	b	n	y	u	e
u	x	b	d	h	y
x	k	f	c	i	u
s	m	p	j	b	r
c	s	h	o	w	v
u	e	s	m	y	e
f	k	n	x	t	p
f	d	l	b	q	s
a	j	n	w	f	u

ZIP = Zone Improvement Plan

Page 48: Keep It Short
3. apartment – apt. 4. Wednesday – Wed. 6. officer – off. 10. producer – prod. 11. singular – sing. 12. literature – lit. 14. Maine – ME 15. Reverend – Rev.

Page 49: Acronym or Not?
4. asap: as soon as possible 5. radar: radio detecting and ranging 8. pin code: personal identification number 10. yuppie: young urban professional 11. laser: light amplification by stimulated emission of radiation 13. modem: modulator/demodulator 16. swat: special weapons action team

Page 50: Collecting Compounds
backfire, firehouse, fireman, flashback, flashlight, headlight, lifetime, lighthouse, nightlife, night-light, nighttime, backlight, headboard, backboard, backfire, outback, outhouse, time-out If students found others, have them share with their classmates!

Page 51: All About Analogies
2. go; 3. told 4. toe 5. spoon 6. orchard 7. japan 8. hive 9. column 10. sun 11. arrow Bonus: hurricane (yolk is the center of an egg, eye is the center of a hurricane)

Page 52: One Word, Two Meanings
2. roll 3. book 4. cast 5. spot 6. well 7. raise 8. fan; 9. bear 10. star 11. fluke 12. wound

Page 53: E-mail Order
Correct alphabetical order is as follows:
m10@cyberplanet.com
mm01@cyberama.com
mmo1@cyberzoo.com
mm12@cyberscape.com
mm12@cyberspaceship.com
mz@cyberfuse.com
mmm123@cybertek.com
mmm1234@cybertek.com
mnm1@cyberquak.com
mnm1@cyberstorm.com
mnn02@cybercafe.com
mon02@cyberinc.com
moo01@cyberocity.com
moo1@cybersimple.com
moo1@cybershow.com

Page 54: Alphabetical Anarchy
2. third letter 3.fourth letter 4. sixth letter 5. ninth letter 6. fifth letter 7. second letter 8. seventh letter 9. third letter 10. first letter

Page 55: Pages From the Dictionary
The following words would not appear between the guide words:
2. kelp 3. holler 4. perpetrate 5. addendum 6. puppet 7. disgruntle 8. white 9. endless 10. quibble

Page 56: Fun With Fə net′ tiks
Phonetic matches should be as follows (phonetic spelling is in parentheses): **Grid 1** – phony (fō′nē); phone (fōn); fan (fan); fine (fīn); funny (fun′ē) **Grid 2** – story (stôr′ē); stir (stûr); store (stôr′); starry (stär′ē); stare (stâr) **Grid 3** – herb (ûrb); hair (hâr); hire (hī r); hero (hēr′ō); hairy (hâr′ē)
Source: Phonetics taken from *Microsoft Bookshelf 2000*

Page 57: Dots in the Wrong Place
1. as·sem·bly 2. au·di·to·ri·um 3. caf·e·te·ri·a 4. el·e·men·ta·ry 5. ex·am·i·na·tion 6. grad·u·a·tion 7. gym·na·si·um 8. prin·ci·pal 9. e·lim·i·nate 10. hi·er·o·glyph·ics 11. pe·di·a·tri·cian 12. cho·re·og·ra·pher 13. re·con·sid·er 14. met·a·mor·phic 15. so·phis·ti·ca·ted

Page 58: Syllable Wizardry
1. n: e·ven, 2. a or y: a·sleep, sleep·y 3. n, a, or r: ris·en, a·rise, ri·ser 4. e: e·rode 5. o: ro·de·o 6. y: man·y 7. a: a·re·a 8. t, f, or c: ta·ble, fa·ble, ca·ble 9. l: cam·el 10. o: ca·me·o
If students found other answers, great! Have them share them with the class.

Page 59: Alphabet Soup
ampersand; apostrophe; asterisk; bracket; parenthesis; question mark; quotation mark; semicolon; seven hundred eighty-nine; thirty-six; two hundred fifty-eight; zero

Page 60: First Words
According to *Random House Webster's College Dictionary,* the following words should be circled because they came into use first in the English language:
1. oven 2. bicycle 3. clock 4. monkey 5. snowball 6. fingerprinting 7. adobe 8. noun 9. song 10. sorceress 11. baseball 12. black